WORKJOBS...FOR PARENTS
ACTIVITY - CENTERED LEARNING IN THE HOME

MARY BARATTA-LORTON

A SELECTION OF ACTIVITIES FROM WORKJOBS

ACTIVITY-CENTERED LEARNING FOR EARLY CHILDHOOD EDUCATION

 ADDISON-WESLEY PUBLISHING COMPANY

Menlo Park, California • Reading, Massachusetts • London • Don Mills, Ontario

This book is in the
ADDISON-WESLEY INNOVATIVE SERIES

Photographs by William Skeahan

ISBN 0-201-04303-3
OPQRS-AL-89876

Dear Parents,

   During the past several years I have been making learning tasks for the children in my classroom built around a single concept I wanted my class to work with. These manipulative activities are designed to help children develop language and numbers skills, as well as more general skills such as hand-eye coordination, observing, seeing relationships, and making judgments. The children in my classes called the activities their "work" or their "jobs." One day a child put the words together as a joke — and it stuck.

   When I published a book of workjobs for other teachers to make for their classes, parents were very enthusiastic about the ideas and many started making these activities for their children to use at home. Because of this interest, I have selected those activities from the original classroom edition of WORKJOBS that seem to be the most appropriate for parents to make and use at home. I hope you will enjoy making and using them with your child.

Sincerely,

Mary Baratta-Lorton

WORKJOBS... FOR PARENTS
ACTIVITY - CENTERED LEARNING IN THE HOME

Contents

WORKJOBS IN ACTION AT HOME: A GLIMPSE

Traci has ten babyfood jars with slits cut in the lids so coins can be dropped into the jars like piggy banks. Traci's mother shows her a quarter and they talk together about different ways to make 25 cents. They discuss the different possibilities of combining coins that still end up with 25 cents worth and then Traci finishes by herself. Her mother goes about her work in another room until Traci is finished and calls her to check her work.

"One, two, three, four, five, nickels. That's a quarter, huh, Mom? Five, ten, fifteen, twenty, twenty-five cents."

Randy and his mother sit together on the couch with the sock boxes. Each sock box has a different item in it which Randy describes one at a time to his mother. His mother looks through the pictures and selects the one thats matches his description.

Randy: "It's long and sharp." Mother: "Is it a nail?" Randy: "It's bigger than a nail and you can write with it." Mother: "A pen?" Randy: "It's made of wood." Mother: "It's a pencil!"

Janet and Billy have dumped a box of buttons onto the floor and are sorting them by color. They put the black buttons together, the pink buttons together, the blue buttons together, and so on.

Robin gets out the sound boxes. Her little brother Robbie and her mother are watching as she works. Robin takes one can and shakes it. She picks up another can and compares the sound it makes with the original can. When Robin finds two cans whose sounds match, she places them as a pair on one of the papers.

"These two are tricky. They sound almost the same."

"That's the sixth pair that match."
"Three more pairs to go."

3

Geoffrey and his father get out the lock board to work on. Geoffrey unlocks a lock, takes off the padlock, and opens the door. Behind each door is a surprise picture: his own, one of a friend or relative, or of a familiar cartoon character. Geoffrey reminds his father of the making of the lock board — how his father let him help screw in the screws and about how Uncle Mark gave them three old padlocks. They talk together about the keys. Some are gold and others silver, some have "teeth" on both sides and others only on one side, some have numbers or animals printed on them and others are plain.

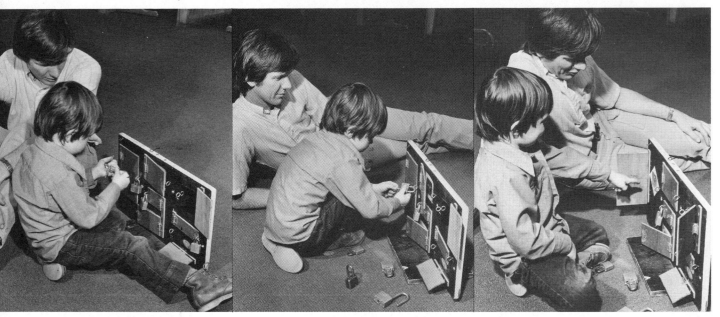

"One of these keys fits, Daddy. I bet it's this one."
"Look Daddy, a picture of Donald Duck."

As Robin was putting away her sound boxes her little brother, Robbie, decided he would like to try the game. Robin thought it would be too hard for Robbie but her mother suggested they take out only a few of the cans and let Robbie try the game. Robin thought that was a good idea and set out three pairs of sounds — the bells, the rice, and the "moo" toys — that would be easily distinguishable from one another.

Shake, shake; rattle, rattle. "Not the same, Mama."

Robbie takes two cans and shakes them at the same time. His mother helps him to shake first one and then the other so he can compare the two sounds. Robbie catches on quickly and finds the first match. When Robbie finishes all three pairs, they decide to leave out these six cans for Robbie to play with during the day. They suggest that in a few days when the game is easier for Robbie they will add another pair of cans.

Steven has the empty jars and lids his mother and a neighbor friend saved. He takes one lid at a time from the box and screws it onto the appropriate jar. Steven has done this several times before and his mother watches with interest, noticing that Steven now predicts correctly for almost all the jars and lids — the first jar he picks up matches the lid. She recalls the first time he did the activity; he frequently picked up a jar that was too small or too large for the lid in his hand and only seemed to find the correct jar by trial and error. Steven had played with this game several times on his own since then and with experience had gotten good at sizing up the correct jar and lid with his eye. He no longer has to rely on trial and error to select a jar.

"This one's right. Now I have nine lids on and I have three more to put on."

Patty and her friend take turns blindfolding one another and trying to put the appropriate screw into the holes of the bolt board. Patty has the blindfold on now and has a large bolt in her hand. She feels with the opposite hand and tells her friend, "This one is too small, I need a big hole. This one must be the right size." She feels the back of the nut and screws the bolt into the hole, feeling it come through with her other hand. They continue to work together until all the nuts and bolts are secured on the bolt board.

"This is a big one; it's easy to turn."

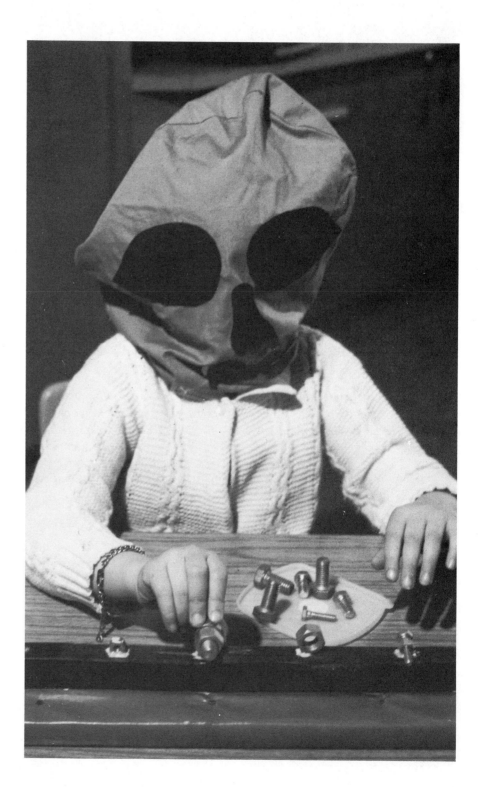

Randy's mother has the bean game out now to show her son for the first time. She asks him to count the number of beans on the first board and then asks him to take off two of the beans. Randy pulls off two of the beans and notices two are still left. He and his mother work together on the other boards and then pop the beans back onto their plastic holder.

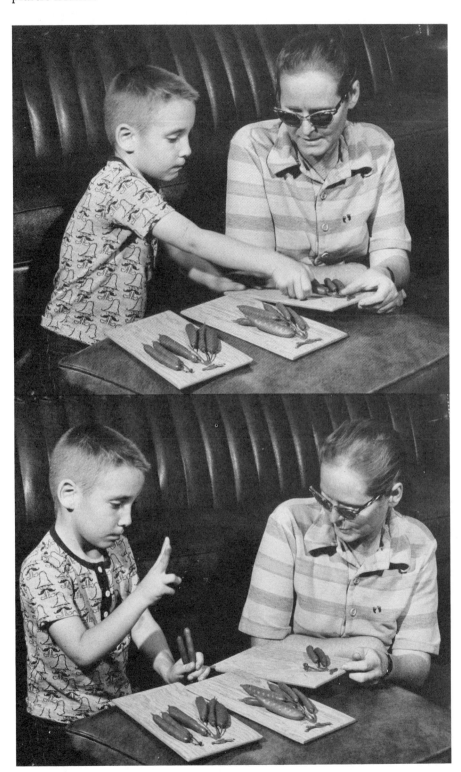

"We have four beans to start with, Randy. Take off two beans."

"And how many are left Randy?"

Steven unscrewed all the lids from the jars and put the jars back into the box. As he began to put the lids away he was telling his mother, "This is the biggest lid. This is the smallest." His mother got an idea from what Steven was saying and asked him to try to put the lids in order. Steven wasn't sure what his mother wanted him to do, so she suggested he find the smallest lid and then the next size larger and so on. When Steven wasn't sure of the size, his mother suggested he put the lid in question directly on top of another lid to see which was larger.

"Which one goes next?"

"This is the biggest lid. It's the twelfth one and it's last."

Billy is now measuring rice into the jars his mother has been saving for him. Some of the jars are short and squat, some are tall and thin. Some have curved sides, others have straight ones. Billy is trying to find out how many cups he has to add to fill up half the jar his mother is holding. Sometimes he loses track and they dump the whole jar out and start over. They continue to work together, sometimes counting the number of spoons of rice it takes to fill the cup or the number of cups to fill a jar. They talk about what the words "full" and "empty" and "half full" mean. They talk about the jar needing a lot or a little more to fill it, and sometimes about a jar having too much.

"How many times do you think you will have to fill up this cup to fill my jar half way, Billy?"

"Let's see how many cups it takes to fill this jar to the top."

9

Geoffrey has gotten out the sink and float game his baby-sitter made for him. He takes a peanut butter jar with a wide mouth and fills it with water. He gets the box of objects and puts them in the water one at a time. If the object sinks, it goes on the sink side, if it floats, it goes on the float side. The wood, the cork, and the boat all float. The jacks and the nail sink to the bottom. Next Geoffrey tries the ball and the paper clip. Geoffrey continues to try the remaining items, proudly showing his father how to play the new game.

"I bet the ball sinks, Daddy. The paper clip goes all the way to the bottom."

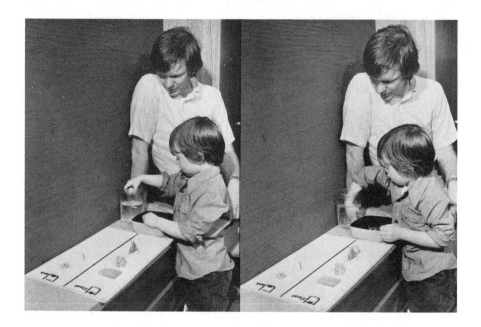

Robin and her father sit on the couch talking about the animal pictures they cut out of old magazines. They go through all the pictures, naming the animals and talking about how the animals are different from one another. Then they go through the pictures a second time, this time placing them according to whether they live mostly in the water, mostly on land, or mostly in the air.

"That's a chipmunk, isn't it Daddy? Look at his fur."

"That's a bear. He lives on land."

Billy and his mother get the cylinder game and find a flat surface to stand the cardboard on. They work together trying to put the lengths of cardboard in order, like stairs. Part way through, Billy's mother realizes that she has too many steps and removes half of the cylinders, leaving Billy with fewer lengths to work with. In other sessions, she may add more steps until he is able to handle them all, but for this first experience a few steps is a good beginning.

11

"Is that the next step Billy?"

Preschool children are creative, resourceful, and imaginative. They are fascinated with objects in the world around them — they squeeze, roll, scratch, pinch, taste, throw, pound, and chew to learn as much as they can about their world. Through this experimentation they learn that some things are soft and bounce, others are hard and break up. Some things taste good, others taste terrible. Some things are bumpy and scratchy, others are soft and smooth. Life is a fascinating world of activity to a young child—a place for doing and discovering and trying things out.

We adults rarely appreciate fully the enormous amount of learning our children achieve through exploration and play before they ever go to school. School too rarely capitalizes on this natural and effective way of learning—exploring and discovering through play.

Through observing children at every stage in the learning process I have found that children learn best when they work with ideas concretely, by handling familiar objects through which they can discover concepts and ideas themselves. Too often children are asked to substitute someone else's experience for their own. The activities in this book are designed with this understanding of the importance of direct experience in mind. Through these activities you can help your child learn to think for himself, to trust his own judgments and thoughts, and to try things "his way" as an expression of his personal creativity and individuality.

When a child has an interested adult to talk to he is guided to think clearly and has a reason for putting his thoughts into words. In time, because of the accumulated experience of translating his thinking into words and answering and asking questions, a child gains in self-expression and consequently feels increasing self-confidence. No goal is more important than your child's feeling of self-worth and no skill or understanding will be more important than this. Those few moments of talking, if they are positive and supportive, will make a *real* difference in your child's life.

HOW TO USE THIS BOOK

There are 43 workjobs in this book. Each is similar in format and includes: the skills for the activity, the activity itself, how to get it started, ideas for follow-up questions, a picture to illustrate the activity, and a materials list. Most of the materials used with the workjobs can be found around the house or at the dime store. You will notice that in the materials lists items are suggested that would make the workjobs more durable. I often suggest that pictures be backed with cardboard and covered with clear contact paper, or that spray paint be used. You will certainly want to use your judgement as to whether your children's use of the workjob will require these precautions. Likewise, sometimes you will want to make a simpler setup for a workjob than is shown in the picture. For example, in The Feely Board (page 40), you may choose not to glue the materials to cardboard or in The Beans (page 104), you may feel that you don't need the plywood board.

The following questions are ones that parents have asked me as they began to make activities to use at home. I include the suggestions I have made to parents in the hope of answering your questions as you begin.

What's the best way to use these activities?

The answer to this question is best answered by *you*. There is no one formula that will work for every parent or teacher. Some parents make five or six activities as Christmas presents and their children use them as they do their toys. Other parents get together with several neighbors and each make four or five activities they can trade each month. Still other parents use the ideas to make activities for their child's nursery school, kindergarten, or first grade classrooms. *Do whatever appeals to you personally.*

The same answer goes for how much time a day or week you should spend with your child working with an activity. The only rule of thumb seems to be to keep it short and fun. A good place to start seems to be with two or three 20-minute sessions per week. Work out whatever is right for you and your child. And remember, it isn't necessary that *you* always be the one who works with your child. A grandparent or older child will often gladly take the responsibility and will enjoy the experience.

At what age should I introduce an activity to my child?

There is no magic formula to this question. No one can tell at what age your child will be four feet tall, and no one can tell the time when he will be ready for a particular experience. You will notice that none of the activities have a suggested age listed. You must use your own judgment and make one or two activities that seem reasonable to you.

If you make an activity and it seems too difficult for one of your children and too easy for another, it can easily be modified to be appropriate for both children. Remember in the earlier description, Billy and Janet's mother began to work with Billy on the cardboard cylinders and learned that there were too many steps for her child to deal with? If your child finds a new activity fun and understands what you want him to do, it is the right level of difficulty. On the other hand, if your child seems overwhelmed and confused, it is too difficult. Understanding this, Billy's mother reduced the number of cylinders Billy had to deal with. This made the activity easier and assured success. In another example, Robbie's mother gave him only three pairs of sound boxes to work with rather than all twelve, making the activity more appropriate. As you child gains in confidence and skill you can gradually increase the number of objects he must work with. In this way, you naturally increase the level of difficulty in the activity, insuring success at every step.

What do I do when my child makes a mistake?

"Mistakes" are often not "mistakes." The longer I work with children the more I'm amazed at how much they teach *me*. Children look at the world in a fresh way and instead of always assuming the child has made a mistake, I try to concentrate on understanding why a child is thinking the way he is. From this I learn how children think. For example, remember Randy's mother working with him as he used the sock boxes? Randy would try to describe the object he was feeling to his mother and she would try to guess the object from his description. Randy's first description was, "It's long and sharp." From this Randy's mother guessed a nail. That made sense and Randy learned from his "mistake" that he hadn't given enough detail in his description. So he added, "You can write with it." When his mother guessed a pen, he again realized, on his own, that he needed to give more information. Randy gradually clarified his description, and understood intuitively the need to include greater detail and refinement in his description. Finally he said, "It's made of wood." This enabled his mother to guess the item he had, a pencil.

The patience and interest which Randy's mother showed gave Randy confidence in his ability and eventually he was able to describe the object completely. She could have shattered his confidence had she not been patient. For example, she could have cut off Randy's thinking by judging him at the start and saying, "That's not enough information." Instead, she guessed from the information given and waited with interest to see what Randy would do when she guessed an incorrect object.

A *child's* thinking can actually expand *our* thinking. I remember one time when I was working with several children with some large geometric shapes. We were naming the shapes: a square, a triangle, and so on. One child looked at the octagon with its eight sides and said it was a diamond. Because there was no "diamond" on the table, I put two triangles together and began to explain that the outline of this shape was referred to as a "diamond". The child obviously didn't like my explanation, and so I asked him to explain himself. He told me that the previous evening his mother had let him look closely at her engagement ring and he noticed the top cut. Indeed, the octagon was a "diamond".

So, when working with what appears to be a mistake, be sure to ask your child about his thinking rather than assuming that he is wrong and needs correcting. There are many different ways of thinking and if your child can explain himself, he is right.

What about storage?

Save all your old boxes from presents and if you know someone getting married soon, have them give you the boxes from their wedding presents. I buy strapping tape from the stationary or hardware store and tape the corners of all the boxes *before* they get broken. I also try to have a separate box for the different parts of an activity and this encourages the children to keep the activity neat.

For the activity Cars and Garages, without the proper container the cars might be dumped into the larger box along with the garages.

The simple addition of a box for the cars ensures the activity will be put away neatly. It is more natural to put things carefully away when there is a special place for everything.

15

If you can find an empty shelf somewhere, the children can keep the things there. Some parents have used the space under the bed as storage. They cut a big box down to about 5 inches and then put several boxes of activities in it and use it as a "drawer" under the bed.

Are the questions for follow-up discussion really necessary?

When we talk to our children, it provides them an important opportunity, a *need*, to express something with words. It is not easy for us to be patient when listening to a child who has difficulty expressing himself. Our natural response is to expect more of children than they are able to give and to expect them to make enormous strides all at once. We must be sensitive to our children's needs and level of language development, and be patient enough to allow our children time to grow. We all learn at different rates because we are individuals. It would be just as absurd to blame a child for not yet weighing 50 pounds by the time he is five years old as it is to blame a child for not yet understanding how to make change or tell time or express himself clearly. We can learn to look at our children objectively, like a television camera, merely seeing, hearing, and recording what we observe, rather than labeling or evaluating what we see. If you keep a record at six-month intervals of your children describing the house they live in, you can really observe your child's growth in language by comparing what he says at a later stage to an earlier one.

ONE LAST NOTE:

The time spent with a child should be enjoyable both for the adult and the child. If you find you have difficulty being patient and understanding when working with your child, be reasonable. Realize that it is only beneficial for you to work with your child if it is going to be fun and bring you closer together. Don't worry if you find teaching is not for you. It certainly doesn't mean you are a bad parent. Simply find someone else, a baby-sitter or older child or grandparent who can spare a little time. You can still have the fun of making the activities for your child to use. Remember, nothing is more important than providing positive and accepting experiences for your child through which you grow closer together. These times are precious — enjoy them.

16

Jars and Lids

Skills Observing size relationships; developing hand-eye coordination; developing small muscles; learning to twist and untwist; learning to make predictions; making comparisons.

18

The child puts the lids on the jars. The task is self-checking: there are twelve jars and twelve lids. If the child puts the wrong lid on one of the jars, he will have a lid left at the end that does not fit the remaining jar.

Children enjoy timing themselves with a stopwatch to see how long it takes them to replace all the lids on the jars. A child can keep track of his best time and compete with himself to improve his time.

Children also enjoy measuring around the widest part of the jar with a piece of string and comparing this length to the jar's height.

ACTIVITY

You might say to the child, "Can you put these together?"

GETTING STARTED

Antoinette, look at this lid for a minute. Do you think it could fit on this jar? Why not? Do you think this one is too small too? How about this one? Try it and see. Good!

Show me a lid that you think would be much too small for this jar. Show me one you think would be much too big. Now show me one you think would be just about right.

Show me the jar with the biggest lid. Well, that's the biggest *jar* for sure, but which jar has the biggest *lid?*

Which jar has the smallest lid?

Show me how you put on this lid. What do we call that motion? What about if you take it off? What do we call the motion?

How many jars are there? How many lids? Are there more jars than lids?

What are these jars made of? What are the lids made of?

IDEAS FOR
FOLLOW-UP DISCUSSION

Twelve jars with lids, each of a different circumference.
Container for the lids.
Container for the boxed lids and the empty bottles.

MATERIALS

Button It Up

Skills Developing small-muscle and hand-eye coordination; learning skills for dressing and undressing; to snap, button, hook, zip, tie, and buckle.

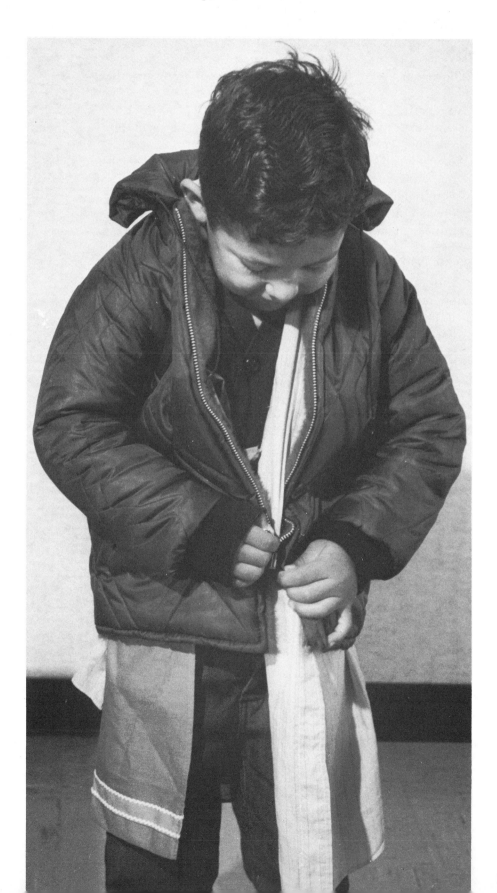

20

The child selects an article of clothing and puts it on over his regular clothes and fastens it closed. For example, if he chooses the shirt which has hooks and eyes, he hooks the shirt closed. (A large mirror, full length if possible, should be available for the child to use during the process.) Then he puts the next one on over the first, and so on, until all are on. A child who is very confident may like to attempt this task while blindfolded.

You might ask, "Which outfit would you like to put on, David? Put on all the clothes—one on top of the other—and fasten them closed."

Tell me about what you did, David.
What do you call this type of clothing?
How many other shirts/dresses are there in this box?
How many are there altogether? *Counting* this one you have on?
What color is the shirt you have on?
What do you call this pattern?
How does the shirt close? How about this dress?
Do you have anything to wear at home with snaps on it? What? Can you fasten them yourself?
Which piece of clothing do you like best? Least?
What color is the dress with stripes? The shirt with checks?

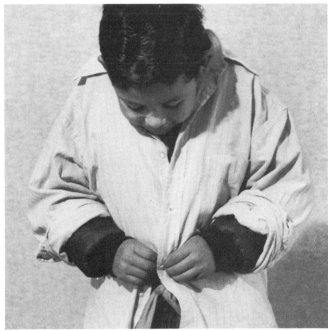

One pair of shoes large enough that a child can put them over his own shoes and lace them.
Shirts and dresses slightly larger than the child, with various closings including buttons, hooks, snaps, belts, zipper.
Container for the clothes.

Note: It is especially good to have two types of zippers—one a skirt-type zipper and one a jacket-type, which is particularly difficult for young children to learn to zip.

The Rice Game

Skills Measuring: making comparisons and seeing relationships; making judgments; developing hand-eye coordination.

The child pours the rice into the jars, being careful to stop filling each jar at the line marked by the rubber band.

Some children will enjoy counting the number of scoops of rice it takes to fill each jar. They can record the number of scoops on a small piece of paper placed in front of each jar. After all the jars are filled the child might order them from the one containing the least amount of rice to the one with the most.

You might say, "See if you can fill the jars up to the line exactly!"

Tell me about your work, Janice.
What exactly did you do?
Which jar do you think has the most rice in it? The least? What makes you think so?
Are there any jars that have the same amount of rice?
What color rubber band is on the jar that is half full?
Do you remember which jar was the first one you filled? The last one?
What do we call this food?
Pour the rice out of this bottle and find out how many cups there are.
Would you like to do it for these others, and write down how many cups you used in all? How would you go about it?

Assorted glass jars and bottles (about ten) of varying sizes and shapes.
Colored rubber bands glued to different levels on the containers.
2 to 6 lb of rice, depending on the size of the jars and bottles used.
Plastic dishpan for the rice.
Funnel.
Scoop or long-handled measuring cup.
Container for jars.

Note: It also is a good idea to place the lid of a large box (as a blanket box) under the jars to catch spills. Have the child fill the jars *in* the dishpan and then set them aside.

You may want to vary the rice game by coloring some of the rice. This can be done by shaking a cup of rice in a jar along with 1½ tablespoons of rubbing alcohol and a squirt of food coloring.

Hook Board

Skills Experiencing one-to-one correspondence; developing hand-eye coordination; strengthening the small muscles used in writing; working with various sizes and distinguishing among them; making comparisons.

The child hangs the washers on the hooks. (A similar hook board may be made with one size hook and the child can form patterns with washers of different sizes and colors.)

ACTIVITY

You might say, "Put one circle on each hook, Lisa." (The child should be left free to discover the possibility of placing the metal washers on the hooks by size.)

GETTING STARTED

What did you do with the metal circles, Lisa?

Tell me about the different sizes you see. Are all the circles the same size? Are *any* of them the same size? Take all the circles off the hooks and put all the same sizes together.

Trace around some of the circles on a piece of paper and try to use the circles as part of your picture. Try it and see how it turns out.

IDEAS FOR
FOLLOW-UP DISCUSSION

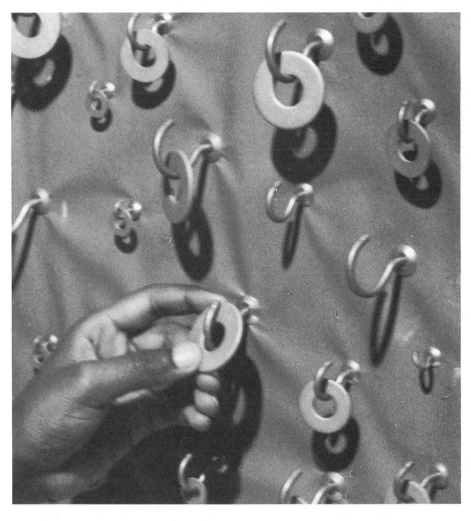

MATERIALS

Plywood, 12″ x 16″.
Piece of wood nailed to the edge of the plywood to make it stand up.
Spray paint or cloth to cover plywood.
Brass cup hooks of various sizes: 10 small, 10 medium, and 10 large.
Metal washers: 10 small, 10 medium, and 10 large.
Container for the metal washers.

The Outline Game

26

The child takes the objects out of the box one at a time and names the item. He then tries to place the object on its outline in only one trial.

Children who are very confident may like the challenge of attempting to reproduce the arrangement *off* the answerboard.

ACTIVITY

You might discuss the activity as follows: "Can you find what shape this flag is on the answerboard? Why do you choose this one? Good thinking! Try it and see. Does it fit? Good. Find where all the objects go."

GETTING STARTED

What did you do with the objects, Christopher?
How did you know where they would go on the answerboard?
Point to an object that is round. Point to one that is made of rubber.
How many objects are green? How many are *not* white, *not* red, or *not* brown? Show me.
What kind of material is this block made of? This bobby pin?
Show me something used to hold things together.
Show me something that cuts.
Point to an object that unlocks a lock.
Would you like to make a book of shapes? Find an object and trace around it on this paper. Bring it to me and I'll write the word for the object for you. When you have five pages, we'll put them together in a book.

**IDEAS FOR
FOLLOW-UP DISCUSSION**

Two 12″ x 18″ pieces of tagboard and cardboard.
Colored pencils to color outlines.
Clear contact paper to protect answerboard.
Masking tape to strengthen all edges.
Cloth tape for making hinges between the two sections of answerboard.
Small objects: block, key, chain, book, scissors, buttons, bobby pin, colored rubber bands, toys, paper clips, rings, comb, clothespin, flag, corks, etc.
Container for objects.

MATERIALS

Weight Boxes

Skills Detecting likenesses and differences; making comparisons; matching; developing baric perception; ordering.

28

The child sorts through the weight boxes to find the pairs of identical weight. He puts each pair on a separate answerboard.

A child who has great difficulty might use a simple balance to weigh his pairs, while one who does this workjob easily may be asked to put his pairs in order according to graduated weight.

ACTIVITY

You might say, "See if you can find the pairs that are the same weight and put them together."

GETTING STARTED

What have you been doing?
Which pair of weights is the heaviest? Which is the lightest?
Would a lemon be heavier or lighter than this weight?
Can you find something in the room that is about the same weight as this one?
Pick up two weights and show me the heavier one.

IDEAS FOR
FOLLOW-UP DISCUSSION

Tagboard squares.
Felt marking pen.
Containers of equal size to be filled at different levels with plaster of paris.
Spray paint to hide the plaster level.
Container for cards and weights.

MATERIALS

Note: The difference in the amount of plaster in the pairs should be great enough to be easily detected. One pair can be empty. The next can have 1/4 cup plaster mixed with water. The next can have 3/4 cup plaster, and the next 1-1/4 cup, etc.

29

Sound Boxes

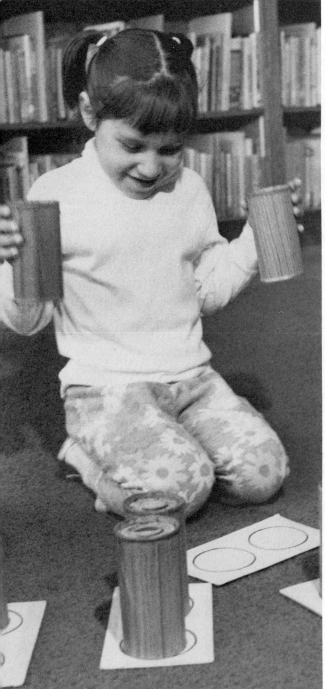

30

The child sorts the containers according to the sound made when he shakes them, placing each identical pair on an answerboard.

You might discuss the activity as follows: "Shake this box and listen to how it sounds. Can you find the box that sounds exactly like this one? Good. Put them together on an answerboard. Can you find another pair?

Tell me how you did your work, Patricia.

Which pair makes the least amount of sound? Which one makes the harshest sound? The softest? Which is the most pleasing to you?

Which pair was the easiest for you to find? Was there one which was hard to find?

What do you think might be in this pair? Could it be rocks? Could it be feathers? Why?

Which pair has a sound which you might hear at a swimming pool, washing dishes, or in the bathtub?

How many pairs jingle?

How can you describe the sounds of these pairs?

Tagboard cut into squares.
Felt marking pen.
Empty orange juice cans or milk cartons.
Two each: ½ cup rice, ½ cup salt or sand, sets of jingle bells, sets of pennies, small balls, 1 cup of water, ¼ cup beans, "moo" toys.
Masking tape to seal cans.
Spray paint.
Container for cards and cans.

The Nail Game

Skills Classifying according to size; developing the ability to think ahead and make predictions; developing the tactile and visual senses; making comparisons.

32

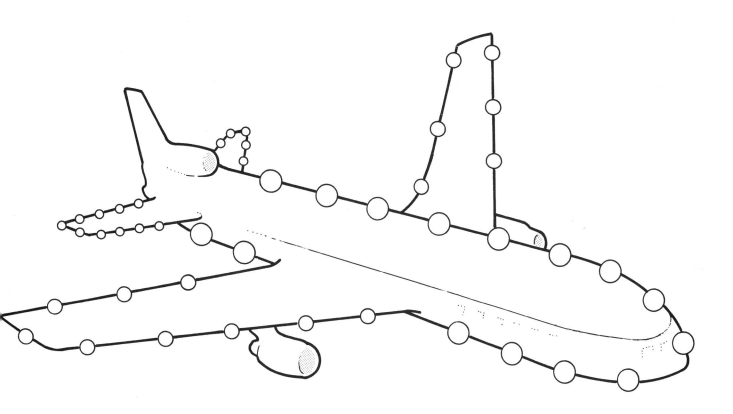

33

A child takes the can of nails and spreads them out on the floor so he can see them. He puts the nails one at a time into the appropriate holes. The task is self-checking: the child ends up with extra nails and the wrong-sized holes if he makes a mistake along the way.

A child who seems to have difficulty with this experience can be given just two sizes of nails to work with at first—the small ones and the very large ones. In this way the child can easily see that there are only two sizes, and prediction will be almost natural.

You might discuss the activity as follows: "See if you can find which hole this nail fits into. Good. What do you think about this one? You're doing fine, Lewis. When all the holes are filled, see if you can see the pattern the nails make."

If a child works for a long time solely by trial and error, you may suggest the following: "Without trying it, Lewis, where do you think that nail might go? Why? Try it and see. Good. How about this nail? What size is it? Are there any nails already in the board that are the same size? Where? Where do you think your nail might go? Why? Try it and see."

Tell me how you put the nails in the board. Did you see any pattern as you were doing it? Was there any way you could tell just by looking at the nail where it was going to go? How?

Show me a small nail. Show me a large nail. Show me a nail in between those sizes. Why is the large sized nail in the wood the same height (just as tall) as the small sized one? How can that be? What makes this one small and this one large? Is it still large when it is *in* the wood? Why?

What shape do the nails outline? What part do the small nails make? What part do the medium ones make? The large?

Piece of wood at least 3-½" thick and 8" x 16" with airplane outline (see page 33 for pattern; this may be traced on the wood, using carbon paper).
15 small nails (1-¼") with heads.
15 medium nails (2-¼") with heads.
15 large nails (3-¼") with heads.
Hand or power drill with small, medium, and large bits to match the nail sizes.
Container for the nails.

Note: Several pieces of wood may be glued together to attain the needed thickness. Also, because the child will use only his fingers to insert the nails, the holes must be big enough so the nails drop down easily and can be easily lifted out. They should be drilled to whatever depth is necessary so that the heads are all at the same level.

Sock Boxes

Skills Identifying shapes through touch; associating form and object; stimulating the imagination; making selections.

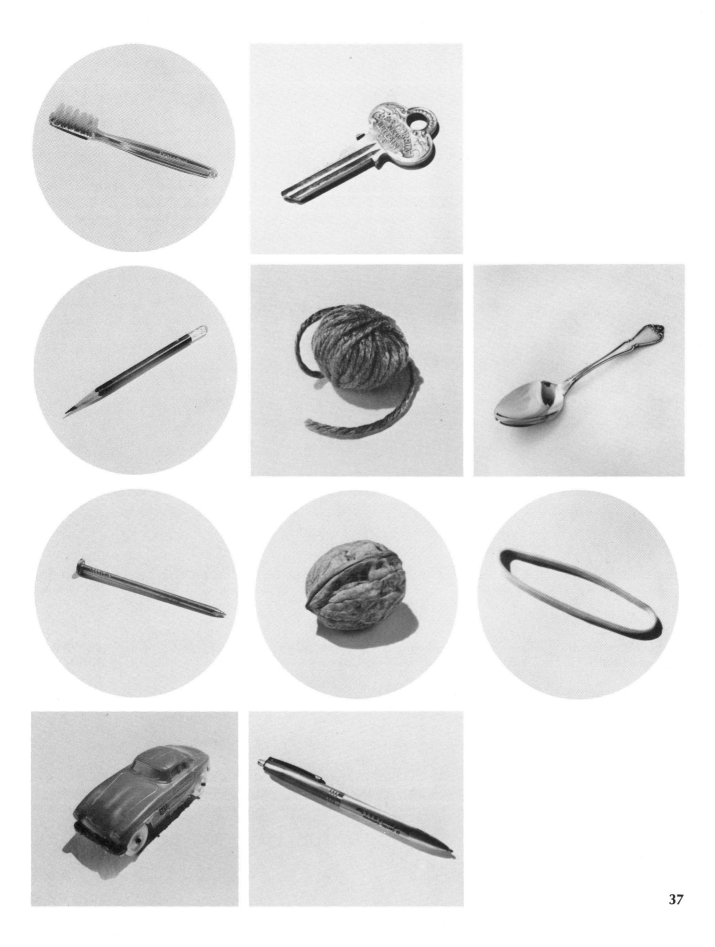

The child puts his hand into the sock box and feels the item inside. Then he sorts through the pictures to find the one that matches what he feels inside the box and places it on top of the sock box. He repeats this procedure for each box, feeling each item, but never looking at it.

ACTIVITY

You might discuss the activity as follows: "Put your hand inside and feel what's there. Can you find a picture of what you feel and put it on top of the box?"

GETTING STARTED

What did you find inside the sock boxes? Can you remember without looking at the pictures?
How many boxes are there altogether?
How did this feel? And this?
Show me something that felt soft. Rough. Tickly.
Can you tell me what color this is by feeling? Why not?
Which thing was the nicest one to feel? Why?

IDEAS FOR FOLLOW-UP DISCUSSION

Children who are ready may label the objects with words rather than pictures.

10 socks.
10 quart-sized plastic containers, approximately 4" tall, stuffed into the socks.
10 objects to be placed in socks (key, pen, pencil, toothbrush, nail, walnuts, toy car, large rubber band, spoon, small ball of yarn).
10 pictures, backed with cardboard and covered with clear contact paper, of the objects placed inside the socks. (See page 37 for pictures to cut out.)
Container for sock boxes and boxed pictures.

MATERIALS

Note: For ease of checking, a code such as the first three letters of the name of each object can be written on a strip of masking tape and placed on the outside of each box. This enables the teacher to check the pictures without reaching into each sock.

The Feely Board

Skills Developing tactile perception; making selections using only the sense of touch; feeling similarities and differences; describing textures; matching.

40

Wearing a blindfold, the child matches each card to its mate on the answerboard by feeling the textures.

You might say, "I'll tie the blindfold on you. Now, see if you can find the pair that matches this card on the answerboard."

Tell me how some of these things feel.

Show me something bumpy. Something smooth. Something that stretches.

Can you tell by *smelling* this material how it will feel? How about if you *look* at it?

How many things feel good to you? Is there anything you don't like to feel? Why?

Where is the thing blind people read? Do they read it with their eyes? Why not? What do they use?

Would this feel any differently if you felt it with your feet instead of your fingers? Try it and see. Would you like to work with a partner and do the game again, feeling with your feet?

18″ x 24″ tagboard and cardboard.
Two identical sets of materials glued to 3″ x 5″ pieces of heavy cardboard; one set then is glued to the answerboard:

elastic	packing plastic	sandpaper	wire screening
macaroni	air bubble	heavy plastic	satin
velvet	sponge	corrugated paper	braille

Container for the second set of objects.
Blindfold.

The Nail Board

Skills Seeing patterns and combinations; matching; forming sets of objects; making comparisons; one-to-one correspondence; making selections.

42

A child takes the pins and hammer, and pounds the pins into the answerboard, reproducing the various patterns.

You might discuss the activity as follows: "Look at this first pattern, Carol. What colors are there? How many of each color? Take that many colored pins. Very good. Now, hammer them into the answerboard making the same pattern as you see here. Very good. Try another pattern."

Tell me what you did with the pins, Carol.

How did you know what colors to use for each pattern? Show me, please.

Point to a pattern that has three red pins in it. What other color pins does it have?

Show me a pattern that has all green pins. Is there any other pattern that has all the same color pins in it?

Show me a pattern that does not have any red pins in it.

Tell me how many pins there are altogether in some set that has red and yellow pins.

I am looking at a set that has five pins altogether, and three of the pins are green. Which one might it be? What color are the other two pins?

Do you have a favorite pattern? Why do you like it? Does it have your favorite color in it? What is it?

12″ x 24″ insulation board, cork, or bulletin material.
Colored marking pens for coloring patterns.
Cloth tape to strengthen all edges.
Colored pushpins, as needed to complete the patterns.
Small hammer.
Container for the hammer and pins.

Float and Sink

Skills Developing the ability to categorize; developing the tactile-visual sense; making judgments; experiencing the properties of water; learning that some things float in water and others sink; developing the concept of opposites.

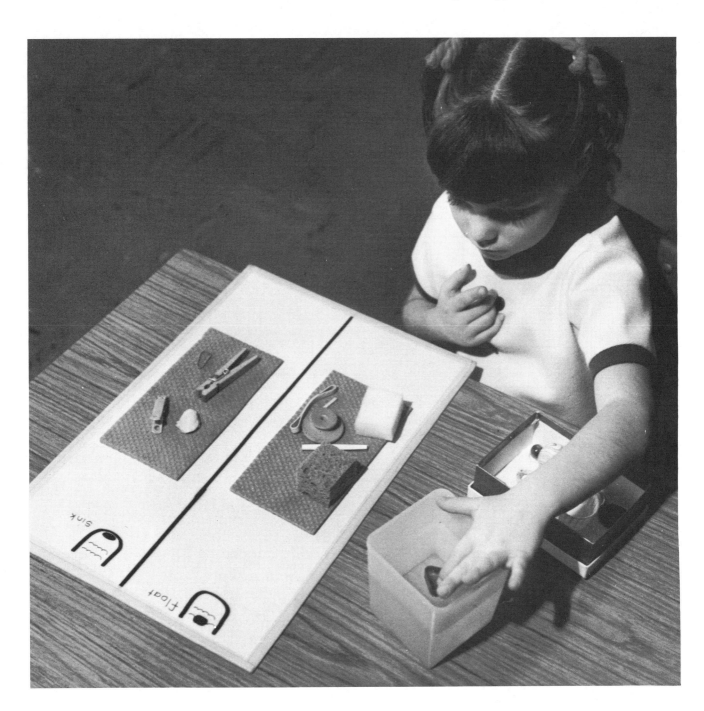

The child fills the water container and, through trial and error, determines whether each object sinks or floats when placed in water. The object is placed on the appropriate side of the answerboard. A mature child may enjoy recording his predictions and his findings.

Children love follow-up activities to the sink and float game where they concentrate on observing the water level when objects are lowered into the container. They mark the original water level on the jar with crayon. Then they try different sized rocks but first estimate by sliding a rubber band around the jar to the level they predict the water will rise to. Then they place the rock in the water and check how close their estimation was. The more experience they have, the more accurate their predictions become!

You might point to the answerboard and say, "This picture shows a container of water like yours. Point to the picture where the object in the water is at the top. Does this object float or sink? Show me the picture where the object is at the bottom. Does it float or does it sink in the water? Good. Now, if you try this object in water and it floats, where will you put it on the answerboard? Why?"

What have you been working with, Gina?

What does this word say? And this one?

Explain the picture on the left side of the answerboard. Why is the picture there? What's it for?

How many objects did you find that would float?

What are these objects made of?

Show me an object that floats. Can you make it sink some way? Try it and see, and then come and get me.

Did more things float or more sink? When you find out, tell me by writing it on the board.

12″ X 18″ tagboard sheet.
Cardboard to back the tagboard.
Clear contact paper for front and back to prevent cardboard from getting wet and warping.
Masking tape to strengthen all edges.
Felt pens.
Assorted objects for experimenting. If possible, some should look identical, but one should float while the other, although similar, sinks—for example, Ivory and Camay guest soaps, and equal pieces of ebony and pine woods.
Container for water.
Thin sponge to catch the water from the objects (to be placed on the answerboard).
Container for objects (lined with contact paper to make it leak proof).

The Button Game

Skills Developing classification skills; sorting according to similarities and differences in color, shape, texture, and size.

The child sorts the buttons into piles. (The child should be encouraged to think of his own criteria by which to sort.)

Several similar workjobs can be made with different sets of buttons. One might have buttons similar in color, style, and size but different in texture. Another set might be buttons of the same color but a different size, or style. Still another might be a random set that the child may sort according to shape or size or whatever criterion he chooses.

A child also could sort by texture if blindfolded. In this case only a few buttons should be included.

ACTIVITY

You might discuss the activity as follows: "Tell me something you notice about these buttons, Isaac." (Color, size, shape, material, number of holes, etc.) "Will you put all the buttons like that together? What will you do with the ones left over?"

GETTING STARTED

Tell me how you grouped these buttons.

Why did you put these buttons here? And here? Could you have put this button here? Why? Why not?

How many buttons are in this group?

If I mixed these buttons up, what else besides their color (or whatever criterion the child has used in sorting) could you tell me about these buttons? How else could you group them?

**IDEAS FOR
FOLLOW-UP DISCUSSION**

Apple crate separator.
100 buttons in matched sets of 5 or 10.
Container for buttons.

MATERIALS

Color Sort

Skills Developing the ability to think in abstract terms; classifying by color; identifying the colors of common objects from memory.

48

The child takes the cards and sorts them according to their colors. Children should be allowed to arrange their groups in any way they wish. Some will work in rows, others in columns, and still others in areas.

By changing the cards at the top of the board you can create different games. For example, the categories might be beginning sounds and the child would sort the cards by their first sounds. Other possible categories might be food, animals, and man-made things or things larger than the child, things smaller than the child and things about the child's size.

You might say, "Put the pictures that are the same color together."

Tell me about the brown things.
Do you have a favorite color? What is the picture, third from the bottom, under your favorite color?
How many yellow pictures are there? Are there more blue ones?
Without looking, can you remember three pictures under the green card? Can you remember three under the red?

Great care should be taken to *ask the child* why he placed pictures the way he did. What is important is that the child have a reason for his placements. For example, he may place the pepper outline under red because that is the color of pepper his mother always uses, or the bananas under brown because he likes to eat them that way, or the apple under yellow or green because he has seen different kinds.

Pocket chart, if available, or spread the pictures out on the floor.
3" x 5" cards.
Outline pictures of objects that are usually a particular color, covered with contact paper and backed with cardboard. (See page 50 for pictures to cut out.)
Rubber cement.
Construction paper squares of eight different colors, glued on tagboard and covered with clear contact paper.
Container for cards and color squares.

53

The Bolt Board

Skills Distinguishing among various sizes; learning to think ahead and make predictions; learning how to screw and unscrew a bolt; developing the tactile and visual senses; developing the small muscles used for writing; making comparisons.

The child screws the bolts into the nuts while blindfolded. The task is self-checking since the child must select the correct sizes of nuts and bolts or he will have some left over. Many children will enjoy the challenge of predicting which bolts go with which size nuts *before* they try them. They can place the bolt they think will fit in front of a nut. Sometimes children want to keep a record of how many of these predictions were correct to see if they improve their record on subsequent trials.

Two children often like to work together on this task with blindfolds on. If a tape recording can be obtained, the teacher can gain important insight into children's thinking and language development.

ACTIVITY

You might introduce the activity as follows: "Choose a bolt from this container, Antoinette. Look at the board. Where do you think it will fit? Here? How about here? You try it and see. Put your fingers in the back of the nut and feel what happens as you screw the bolt through. Very good! Find where each bolt goes and then let me see!"

GETTING STARTED

What did you do with all the bolts, Antoinette?

Are *all* the bolts the same size?

Are *any* bolts the same size? Show me.

Show me a bolt that is small. One that is medium sized. One that is large.

Show me a nut that is *not* on the right side of the board. What side is it on? What size is it?

Are there more small nuts and bolts or more large nuts and bolts? Show me.

Point to a bolt that is not medium sized, and not small sized. What size is it? Where is it on the board?

How many nuts and bolts are there altogether? Count them for me, please.

What happens if you try to put the bolt into the nut from the other side? Will it still screw in? Try it and tell me what you find out.

IDEAS FOR
FOLLOW-UP DISCUSSION

One piece of wood 1″ x 1″ x 3′ glued to a 1″ x 4″ x 3′ board.
Five small nuts and bolts.
Five medium nuts and bolts.
Five large nuts and bolts.
Epoxy glue to glue nuts to the small piece of wood.
Container for bolts.
Blindfold (optional).

MATERIALS

The Screw Game

Skills Observing size differences; making predictions; developing the small muscles used in writing; learning to use a screwdriver to put in and remove screws.

The child screws each metal screw into the correctly sized nut on the board with his screwdriver.

You might ask, "Can you screw these screws into the holes, Charles?"

What have you been working with, Charles?
Tell me what you did.
What are these called?
How did you go about putting the screws into the wood?
Are all the screws the same size, Charles? Tell me about the sizes.
Have you ever used a screwdriver before? What for?
Did you ever see someone else using a screwdriver? What for? Who?

One piece of wood at least 1-1/2″ thick.
A drill for drilling holes into the wood.
Epoxy glue to glue the nuts over the holes in the wood.
15 stove bolts with matching nuts.
A short-handled (4″) screwdriver (much easier for a young child to manipulate than a long-handled one).
Container for screws and screwdriver.

Note: The nuts can be hammered flush with the wood so they will stay firmly in place.

People Pictures

Skills Becoming aware of various feelings; classifying; developing the ability to form judgments; seeing similarities and differences.

A child takes the pictures and sorts them in some way.

Some children will sort in the obvious way—happy and sad. Other children separate all the men, all the women, and all the men and women who are happy or sad. Still others have elaborate schemes for sorting such as *why* the people might feel as they do. If free to do so, most children will think of their own categories.

You might discuss the activity as follows: "Christopher, look at these pictures and tell me about them. Do you remember when you sorted the buttons and the fish and the nuts? How could you sort these pictures into two groups? Are there any pictures that have something the same about them that you could put into one group?"

Tell me about these people, Christopher.

Why did you put all these pictures together here? And these?

How do you think this person feels? What can you think of that might have caused him to feel this way?

Is there a picture that reminds you of some way you once felt? Why?

How might I look if I had just burned my dinner in the oven? Is there a picture that shows someone looking like that?

Is there a picture that would show how you might look if you had just had your new bike stolen?

How about a picture of how someone might look if he had been offered a big piece of cake? Do you like cake? How might you look if you didn't like cake?

Would you like to make a book? Can you find pictures of happy people and sad people (or men and women, or children and grownups, or fat people and skinny people, or whatever the child has been working with) in this magazine?

ACTIVITY

GETTING STARTED

**IDEAS FOR
FOLLOW-UP DISCUSSION**

Pictures cut from magazines, mounted on tagboard, showing a variety of emotions.
Clear contact paper for protecting pictures.
Container for pictures.

MATERIALS

Go-Together Bottles

Skills Associating things that belong to-gether; developing logical thinking; making selections; identifying names of objects.

The child takes the jars with the objects and places them so he can see the objects inside each one. Then he takes the pictures and places them on top of the appropriate jars.

ACTIVITY

You might ask, "What is inside this jar? Can you find a picture of something that goes with it? Would these two things be used together? How about this? What would be used with it?"

GETTING STARTED

How would these two things be used together? Would *you* ever use them? Would your mother?

IDEAS FOR FOLLOW-UP DISCUSSION

Show me something you could use to sew with. Show me something you could write with. Show me something you could burn with.

Show me three things that are black. Show me two things that are red.

Show me something a baby could use. Something you could find in a drawer. Something with legs.

Show me something made of wood. Of plastic. Of metal.

Some children may enjoy matching words to the jars.

MATERIALS

20 baby food jars with lids.
Tape to seal the jars closed when objects are inside.
20 objects:

watermelon seeds	pencil eraser	pop top from soda can	stamp
tire	key	screw	candles
match	water	hollow egg or corn seeds	buttons
safety pin	flower	pennies	stars
needle	peanuts	fishing hook	nails

20 pictures, backed with cardboard and covered with clear contact paper (see page 61 for pictures to cut out):

watermelon	pencil	soda can	letter
toy car	door	screwdriver	cake
fire	bathtub	hen	shirt
baby's diaper	vase	piggy bank	flag
thread	peanuts in shell	fishing pole	hammer

Container for pictures.
Container for boxed pictures and jars.

63

Animal Habitat

Skills Learning about the natural environment of various animals; classifying animals according to their habitat; making comparisons; drawing conclusions.

The child sorts the pictures under the appropriate categories, placing together the animals which live in the water, those which live on land, and those which live in the air.

Parents may want to have several sets of pictures for the children to sort with this answerboard. They might select pictures of vehicles or machinery such as a submarine for "in water," a lawn mower for "on land," and an airplane for "in the air." Another group of pictures could be prepared for uniforms that might be worn in these categories such as a deep-sea diver's outfit for "in water," a football uniform for "on land," and an astronaut's suit for "in the air."

You might discuss the activity as follows: "If an animal lives mostly on the land, where will his picture go? If he lives mostly in the air, where will his picture go? If he lives mostly in the water, where will his picture go? Put the pictures where you think the animals live most of the time."

Name all the animals that live mostly in the water. Those that live mostly in the air, and those that live mostly on the land.
Name an animal that is very small and lives on the land. Name one that is huge.
Do you know the name of the largest bird? The largest animal? The tallest one?
Put all the animals with horns in one pile.
Show me some animals whose names you do not know, and I'll tell you their names.

9″ x 12″ sheets of tagboard, cardboard, and clear contact paper.
Marking pen for drawing habitats.
Cotton for clouds.
Cloth tape for hinging sections of answerboard together.
Pictures of animals that live mostly in the water, mostly on land, and mostly in the air.
Container for pictures and folded answerboard.

Keys and Locks

Skills Developing hand-eye coordination; strengthening memory; perceiving different sizes and shapes; developing the small muscles; observing an orderly sequence.

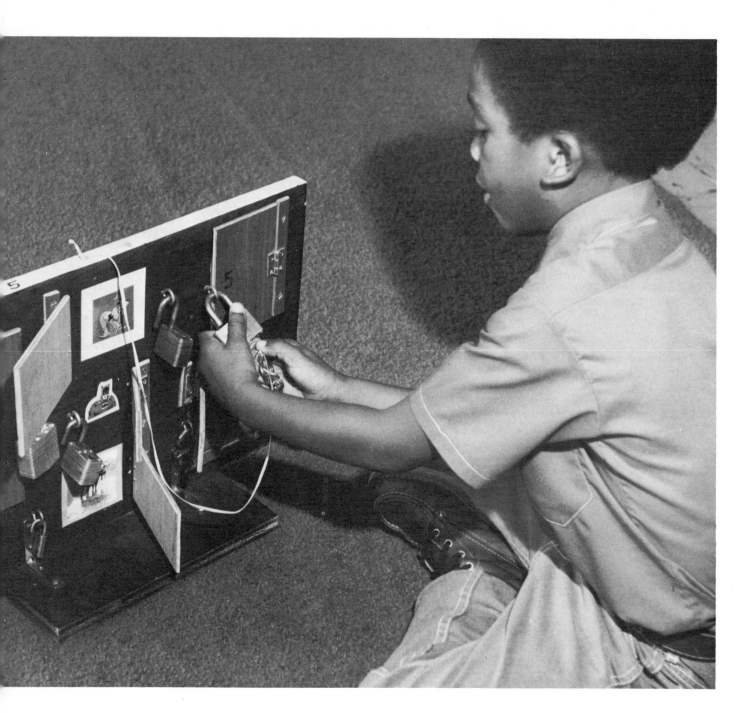

The child unlocks each lock with the appropriate key. When he is finished, he locks each lock and hangs up the keys.

You might say, "See if you can open all the locks!"

Tell me how you did your workjob, Mark.
What are these called? And these?
How many locks are there all together?
Are there more locks than keys?
If I took away this key, would you be able to open *all* the locks?
Do you need the keys to put the locks back on and close them? Try and find out.
Do you have any locks like these at home?
What locks have you been allowed to open at home?
Do we have any locks in this room? See if you can find out how many.

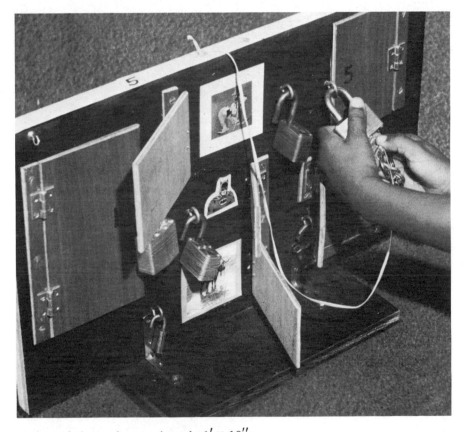

A piece of plywood approximately 1′ x 18″.
Small doors hinged to a strip of wood to be nailed to the plywood.
Rings or fasteners on which to hang the locks.
Assorted locks and keys.
Key chain for keys.
A piece of wood approximately 1′ x 4″ x 6″ to nail to the edge of the plywood to make it stand up.
Hook on which the keys may be hung.
Funny pictures to be glued inside each door.

Note: The difficulty of this workjob depends on the number of locks included. A combination lock can provide a great challenge.

The Cylinders

Skills Making comparisons; observing the relationship of one size to another; ordering by height; making selections; developing visual perceptions; predicting and checking.

The child takes the graduated cardboard tubes and experiments until he has the pieces in an orderly, progressive row.

ACTIVITY

The child should be allowed to experiment to find the best system, for him, for getting the tubes into the desired arrangement. A child with little experience will usually begin haphazardly in the middle and work toward both ends. This same child will soon begin to work from one end, judging with his eye and predicting which cylinder goes next in the series. Each child should be allowed to gain this insight through his own experience.

Pointing to the reference card, you might say, "Arrange the cylinders to look like this pattern."

GETTING STARTED

How did you line the cylinders up?

Which cylinder is the tallest? Is it on the right or left side?

If I take this cylinder away, which one is the tallest? If I take this one away too, is it still the tallest?

How can you make this cylinder the shortest in a series without cutting it shorter?

Can you mix the cylinders up and work backwards, so the little one is on the other side?

Close your eyes. I'm going to do something, and I want you to tell me where the pattern is broken. (You remove a cylinder leaving the others in place. The child points to the space. You repeat but close the space up. Finally mix up the cylinders so the child must rebuild the pattern to find which one is missing.)

IDEAS FOR
FOLLOW-UP DISCUSSION

Cardboard tubing cut into ½" graduated pieces.
Spray paint.
Container for cylinders.
Reference card, glued to container, which shows gradation.

MATERIALS

Syrup Game

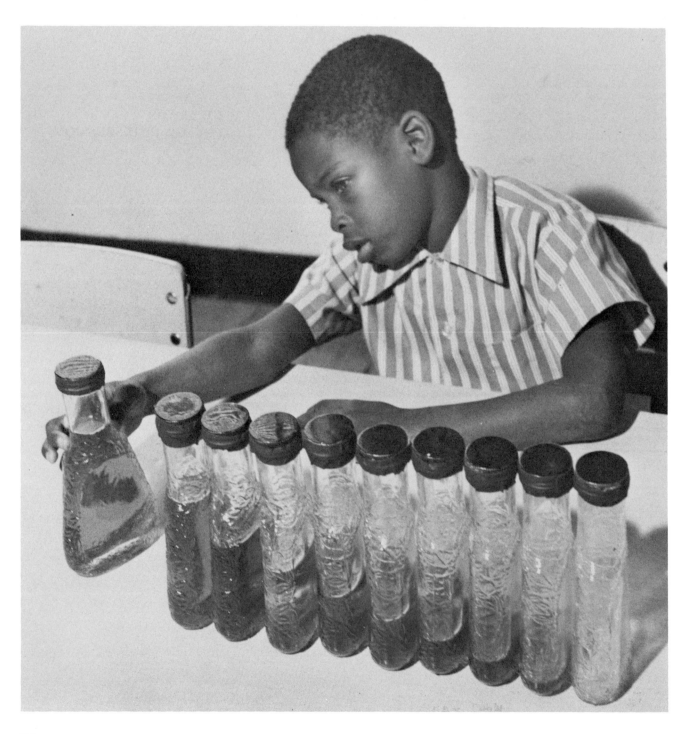

A child takes the bottles of colored water, which have been filled at 1/2″ gradations, and lines them up in order.

The activity might be discussed as follows: "Do you remember the cardboard cylinder game, Tim? This is a lot like that game. Will you arrange these bottles in the same order?"

What can you tell me about the bottles?

If you had all your relatives over to breakfast next Sunday, which bottle would you want to have on the table filled with syrup? Why?

If you were going to have pancakes after school and you were the only one that was going to have them, which size would you choose to be filled with syrup? Why?

Which bottle has the least amount in it? The most? How many are in between? Which ones would you say have a lot? Which ones would you say have just a little bit?

Empty bottles.
Colored water in increasing amounts in each bottle.
Cloth tape to seal bottles.
Tall container for bottles to prevent them from tipping over.

First-Sound Sorting Boxes

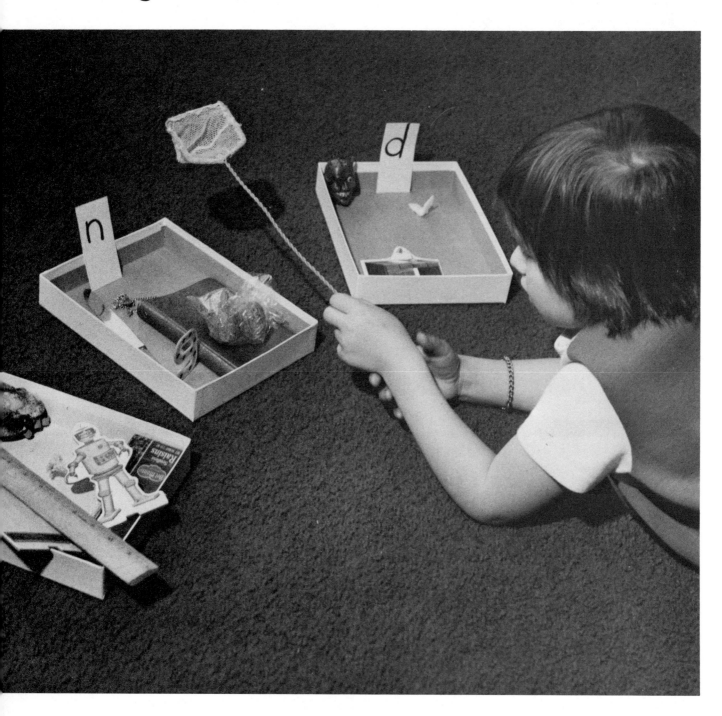

The child sorts the objects into the boxes matching the initial sound of each object with the appropriate letter.

You might discuss the activity as follows: "Pick up one of the objects from the box. What is it? Does that word start like this—'rrrr'—(pointing to the box with the 'r' on it)? Does it start like 'nn' (pointing to that letter)? Does it start like 'd'? Yes! Let's say it together. Can you hear that first sound of 'd'? Put it in the box. Now, take the next object and see if you can find this one yourself."

Say the names of the things in the "nnn" box. Do they all begin with "nnn"?

Show me something beginning with "rrr" that could help a person draw a straight line. Something hard. Something cold inside.

Show me something beginning with "nnn" that you could eat. Something you could mend a rip with. Something you could use to catch a goldfish with.

Show me something beginning with "ddd" you could buy something with.

Three boxes, each designated with one letter.
Spray paint.
Objects to be sorted according to their initial sounds;
   r: rock, ruler, raisins, robot, refrigerator, rocker, rice
   n: net, notebook, needle, nine, necklace, nuts, nail
   d: dove, desk, devil, dog, dime, doll, dish
Container for objects.
Container for boxes and boxed objects.

Supermarket

Skills Developing auditory perception; selecting and reproducing beginning sounds in words; classifying according to first sounds; associating sound and symbol.

74

The child takes the objects and sorts them into the bags according to their first sound.

Pointing to the letters on the outside of the bags, you might ask, "How does this letter sound? And this one? Can you find the objects that will go into each bag? How about this—what is it? Does it begin with this sound? With this one? Then where will you put it? Do the next one while I watch."

Show me something you might eat for breakfast. What sound does it begin with?

Is there something hard? What do you do with it? What is it's first sound?

What do you put on a sandwich? What kind of a sandwich would you use it on? What sound does it begin with?

Show me something that begins with the same sound as Michael's name.

Close your eyes. Name as many things as you can that you put in the "sss" bag. Good for you, Lisa. Now let's check.

Three paper bags with a letter written on the outside.
A series of objects whose names begin with the sounds on the bags.
Container for objects.
Container for the bags and boxed objects.

Note: Similar games can be made for other beginning sounds where the letter is written on an object such as clothing, birds, buttons, or car engines. The child then matches these with corresponding objects such as clothes lines, nests, shirts, or cars which are identified with the appropriate beginning sounds.

Animal Cages

Skills Developing auditory perception; identifying and reproducing beginning sounds in words; associating sound and symbol.

The child says the name of the animal and listens for the beginning sound. He places the animals in the appropriate cages according to the beginning sound.

The children should have an understanding of beginning sounds and be familiar with the names of the animals they will use before they begin this workjob.

You might ask the child, "What is the name of this animal? What sound does it begin with? Can you find the letter which makes that sound and put the animal in that cage?"

Show me an animal whose name begins with the sound of "l".

If I were going to write down the word "rhinocerous," which letter would I write first? How about "tiger"? Or "walrus"?

Name the animals for me.

Show me an animal that lives in the trees. One that loves to swim. One that is very large and heavy.

If I gave you a turtle, which cage would he go in? What if I gave you a cat? A leopard?

One toy animal of each kind: deer, monkey, rhinocerous, lion, tiger, camel, zebra, bear, gorilla, hippopotamus, fox, seal, walrus.

Empty strawberry baskets with one letter affixed to each: *d m r l t c z b g h f s w.*

Container for animals.

Container for boxed animals and "cages."

Note: If three baskets are stacked and taped together the "cages" will be very sturdy.

Cars and Garages

Skills Counting; matching; making comparisons; making selections.

78

The child matches the dots on the car with the numeral on the garage and drives the car into its garage. The car with seven dots should drive into the garage with number 7. The one with only two dots drives into number 2.

The activity might be discussed as follows: "How many dots are on this car? Count them for me, please. How many are there? Can you find a garage that this car can drive into? Why do you think the car goes into this particular garage? Very good. Where do you think this car goes?"

What did you do with the cars?
Why did you drive *this* car into *this* garage?
What is this numeral? How can you show me what numeral it is if I don't know what it is?
If I drove this car (with four dots) into this garage (with numeral 1), would it be okay? Why?
How many cars are there with three dots?

Empty milk cartons cut as shown.
Colorful construction paper covered with clear contact paper.
Numeral cards, hinged, with number dots underneath.
Small plastic cars.
Marking pen for drawing dots on the cars.
Container for cars.
Container for garages and boxed cars.

Easter Baskets

The child fills each basket with the appropriate number of "eggs" and orders the baskets from 1 through 10. When the work has been checked, the child places the cup of cereal in his desk until recess when he may eat it!

A child who is ready may enjoy placing two baskets together and recording the combinations formed.

ACTIVITY

You might ask the child, "How many Easter eggs will you put in this basket? And this one?"

GETTING STARTED

Tell me what you've been working on.

How did you go about doing this work?

Show me a basket that has the same number of eggs as we have doors in our room. Show me a basket that has the same number of eggs as my car has wheels. Show me a numeral that tells how many teeth you have missing in the front of your mouth.

How many eggs do you have in this basket? (Child counts.) What number is on the front of the basket? Are there that many eggs? (If not) Can you fix it so there are that many eggs?

If you eat three eggs from this basket, how many eggs would you have left? Eat them and let's see.

If you dump the eggs in this basket with these others, how many would you have?

**IDEAS FOR
FOLLOW-UP DISCUSSION**

MATERIALS

10 small Easter baskets.
Plastic Easter grass, enough to fill each basket.
White, clear-drying glue to mix with grass before filling baskets so the grass will stick to the basket.
Writing pen for writing numerals.
Small cups of sugar-coated cereal (of different colors) to look like Easter eggs.
Container for baskets.

Hangers and Clothes Pins

Skills Forming sets of objects; counting; ordering numerically.

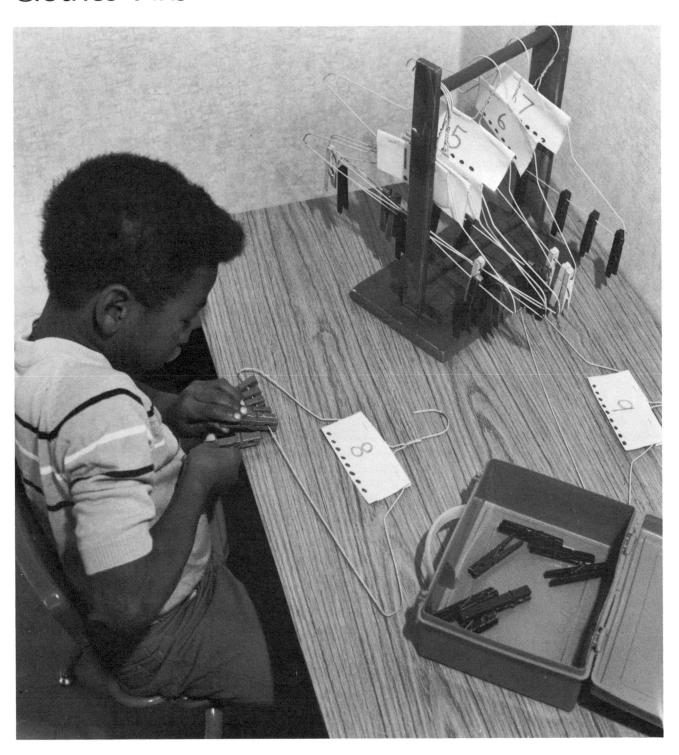

...d puts the appropriate number of clothespins on the hangers ...ders them from 1 through 10.

...ou might ask the child, "How many clothespins will you put on this hanger? And this one?"

Tell me about your work and what you've been doing, Howard.
Why did you put six clothespins on this hanger?
How many red clothespins are on this hanger? How many altogether?
Let's write down how many of each color you have on this hanger.
   First take a red crayon. How many red clothespins are there? Can you write that? (Child writes the number or makes dots or lines depending on his readiness.) And how many yellow pins are there? What color will you use to write that many? And how many green? How many are there all together?
Which hanger has the most clothespins on it? Which one has the least? Which one has the same number as your age? As you have fingers on two hands? As you have noses?

10 clothes hangers.
Colored plastic clothespins or spray painted wooden pins in four colors.
Tagboard cut into 3" x 5" strips covered with clear contact paper after writing numerals.
Stapler to affix numeral cards to clothes hangers.
Something to hang the hangers on.
Container for clothespins.
Container for hangers and boxed clothespins.

Piggy Banks

Skills Forming sets of objects; counting; making comparisons; learning about money; developing respect for property; combining groups.

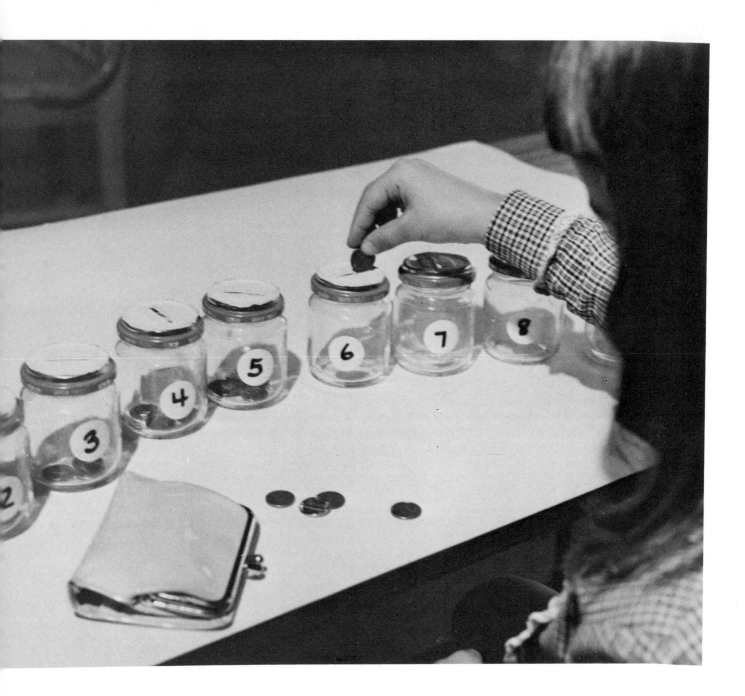

The child drops the appropriate number of pennies or disks into each "piggy bank." For instance, in the bank marked "9" he drops in nine pennies, and in the one marked "3" he drops in three.

You might ask the child: "How many pennies will you put into this bank? Why?"

What did you do with the pennies and jars?
Could you put the banks in order from 1 through 10?
Which bank has the most money in it? The least?
If you wanted to buy a piece of penny bubble gum, which bank would you get the money out of?
If I wanted you to give me six cents from *two* banks, which two would you use? How about eight cents? Four cents?
If you wanted to buy a balloon for four cents, which bank would you take the money from?
Show me a bank that has the same number of pennies as your age.
Count all the pennies and tell me how many there are.

10 baby food jars with lids.
Screwdriver to punch slots in lids.
Sticker numerals glued to jars.
Cloth tape for covering the jagged metal of the slots.
Pennies, poker chips, or other small disks.
Matching board for counting the money.
Container for disks, chips, or pennies.
Container for jars.

The Paper Clip Game

A child clips as many paper clips to each square as the numeral shows him.

When he is able to do so, the child can put two cards together and record the combinations formed.

You might discuss the activity as follows: "How can you find how many paper clips to clip to this square? Good for you! Put on that many paper clips."

What did you do with the paper clips? How did you know how many to put on each square?

Tell me about this card. What does this "3" mean?

This has a mistake. Can you find it yourself and fix it?

Show me a card that has the same number of paper clips as your age. Show me a card that has less than your age. How long ago were you that old? Can you write that subtraction problem and the answer on the board?

4″ x 4″ tagboard squares covered with clear contact paper.
Marking pen to write numerals.
Masking tape to strengthen edges.
Large paper clips.
Container for paper clips.
Container for squares and boxed paper clips.

The 1-10 Train

The child hooks each car onto the train in numerical order from 1 through 10.

You might discuss the activity as follows: "The engine is going to pick up its cars in order. Which one will it pick up first? Can you find that car? What car should come after that one?"

Say each number for me, please. (Looking at a car that is out of order) Let's name the numbers together and see which number should go here. One, two, three, four . . . . What number should this car have on it? Is this the right car? Can you find the one you need and hook it on? Good! And which car will go next?

Which car is between eight and ten? Which car is before four? Before seven? After two?

How many cars are yellow? Green? How many are *not* red or yellow?

Small toy engine and cars that hook together.
Black marking pen to write the numerals 1 through 10 on one side of the train car, and the appropriate number of dots on the other.
Container for toy train.

Bracelets

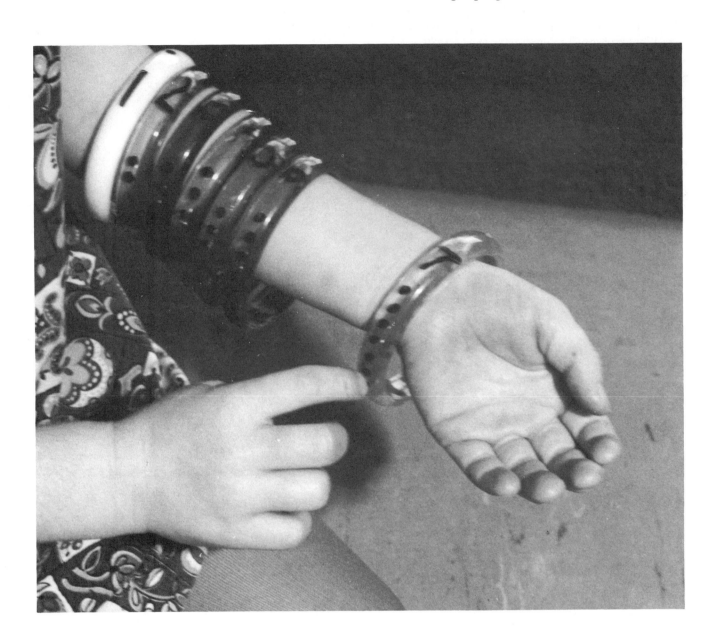

The child takes the bracelets one at a time, starting with number 1, and puts them on his arm in numerical order.

You might ask the child, "Which number comes first when you're counting? Can you find that number on one of the bracelets and put it on? Which one will you put on next?"

Which number comes after six?

Which number is between seven and nine? (Pointing to the numeral on the numeral card and the bracelet that has been put on upside down) Is this number exactly the same as this one? Can you fix it so it looks the same?

How many bracelets are red or yellow? How many can you hold in one hand easily? How many are left over?

I am looking at an orange bracelet. What is the number on it?

I am looking at a bracelet that is between numbers three and five. What color is it?

Without peeking, can you remember the color of bracelet number ten? How about number one?

10 sturdy plastic bracelets.
Marking pen to write numerals 1 through 10 on the bracelets.
Container for bracelets.

Days of the Week

Skills Learning the days of the week; reading; learning about the calendar; reinforcing left-to-right progression.

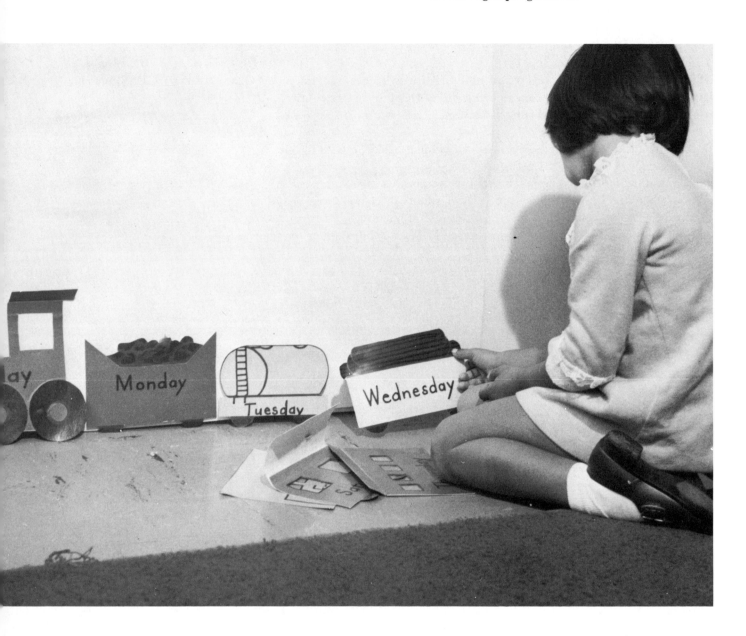

The child places the cards in order, with Sunday first, then Monday, and so forth, to show the days of the week.

Each child should have a calendar for reference as he orders the days of the week. If it is across the room, so much the better, for the child will be strengthening his memory by keeping the word pattern in his mind as he walks back to where he is working.

Similar games can be made for the months of the year or for ordinal sequence, listing first, second, third, and so forth.

The activity might be discussed as follows: "What is the first day of the week? It's the day some people go to church. Yes, Sunday. And which day comes next? Good. Can you put the days after this in order?"

Which day is the first school day of the week? What is the first day of the week?
Which is the last day of the week? What do you do on this day?
How many days are there in a week? How many of these days do you go to school? How many are in the weekend?
Which day of the week begins with a "W"? With an "M"?

Paper for cutting out the outlines of seven train cars.
Black marking pen for writing the days of the week on the cars.
Clear contact paper to protect the train cars.
Pictures of activities done on particular days to be sorted with the appropriate train car.
Container for the train.

Individual Sentence Charts

Skills Experiencing the ability to draw and write about what one thinks and share it with other people; matching words in a sentence; reading; writing practice.

The child draws or paints a picture. You then write at the bottom what the child tells about his picture. The child may try to write under the written words. Later, you write the words from the sentence and put on the tag strip to form pockets. The child then can match the individual words to the words in his sentence and practice reading.

Children can make books of these individual sentence pictures. When they have three or more sentences, they can mix up all the words from the sentences and learn the words individually as well as match them.

ACTIVITY

When your child has finished painting, you might say, "Tell me about your painting. What would you like me to write down about your picture? Good. Read it to me. Would you like to try writing under my writing?" When the child is ready to match the word cards to the words in the sentence, you can say, "Find where these words go in your sentence."

GETTING STARTED

Tell me about your work. What is this at the bottom? Read it to me please.

Which word says "park"? Which one says "car"?

How many words are in your sentence?

Is this sentence you wrote today longer or shorter than the last one you wrote? Show me.

How many letters are in this word?

What do we call this area between the words? What is it for?

What is this mark at the end of the sentence called?

Which is your favorite picture of all the ones you've done? Why?

Mix up all the words from these three sentences, and see how many you can read to me.

IDEAS FOR FOLLOW-UP DISCUSSION

Easel paper.

Paints and brushes for the child to paint pictures.

Marking pen to write the child's sentence as it is dictated.

1″ strip of tagboard taped to the bottom of each picture, making a pocket chart.

Word cards for writing each word of the child's sentence.

MATERIALS

Materials

Skills Learning to read descriptive words; identifying the material of common objects; identifying properties of common materials; labeling; making comparisons.

96

The child sorts the objects under the various categories to show the materials with which each is made.

A child who does this activity with ease may enjoy making a scrapbook of things made of different materials. He can copy one word on each page from the answerboard and paste pictures under the various headings.

You might discuss the activity as follows: "Pick up one of these things and feel the material. Look at it closely. Do you know what it is made of?" (If your child does not know hold the object in front of each word on the answerboard and ask "Is this made of wood?" or, "Is it made of metal?" . . . until the child finds the materials.)

Name all the things made of metal. The things made of wood.
Show me something made of glass that is used at Christmas.
Of what material are the things in the fourth pie tin from the left?
What is the same about things made of glass?
Show me some things that are hard. Some things that stretch. Some things that will break.
Where does leather come from? Rubber? Wood?
Are any parts of your clothing made of metal? Of wood? Of plastic? Of leather?

Six 9″ X 12″ pieces of heavy cardboard taped together.
Marking pen for writing the name of each material.
Small pieces of wood, glass, metal, rubber, plastic, and leather to glue to the answerboard.
Objects made of
  Wood: clothespin, tongue depressor, pencil, button, spool, match, twig, wheel
  Glass: jar, mirror, Christmas tree bulb, flashbulb
  Metal: can, paper clip, screw, nail, bottle cap, metal foil, button, pen, empty film spool
  Rubber: rubber band, balloon, medicine dropper top, ball, rubber cement (sealed shut)
  Plastic: straw, spool, spoon, toothbrush, comb, toy, button, ball
  Leather: wallet, belt, hide, key ring, button, child's shoe
Six metal pie tins.
Container for objects, answerboard, and pie tins.

Alphabet Train

Skills Pairing capital and small letters of the alphabet; selecting first sounds of words; experiencing alphabetical order; strengthening left-to-right progression.

The child takes the objects and puts them into the alphabet train according to their beginning sound. The "cat" goes into the car marked "c," the rat goes into the one marked "r," and so forth.

You might discuss this activity as follows: "Choose one object from the box. What is it? What sound does it begin with? What letter does it begin with? Can you find that letter on the alphabet train? Yes, there it is! What about this next object?"

What word starts with the letter "s"? The letter "c"? The letter "m"?
What sound does "fork" begin with? Where would a "man" go in the alphabet train? Where would a "pen" go?
How many letters are there in the alphabet? How many letters are after "s"? After "x"?
What letter comes between "a" and "c"? Between "n" and "p"?
Show me a short letter. A tall one. A wiggly one. A straight one. One with a dot over itself.
Name two letters at the beginning of the alphabet. One at the end.
Show me all the letters that are in your name.

26 milk cartons cut down as shown.
Colored paper in various colors to cover the cartons.
Clear contact paper to cover the colored paper.
Marking pen to write the letters of the alphabet on the cars.
Small cardboard circles for wheels.
Brass fasteners to attach wheels to cars.
Yarn to link the 26 cars together.
Engine.
Two or more objects beginning with each sound of the alphabet to go inside the train car; for example, *a*pple, *a*nchor, *b*ed, *b*one, *c*at, *c*ar, *d*oll, *d*uck.
Container for objects.
Container for train and boxed objects.

Math Recording Game

Skills Forming sets of objects; counting; learning to record experience with mathematical symbols; reading; making comparisons.

The child records with pictures and words what he sees on each answer-card, and fills in the missing numeral.

You might discuss the activity as follows: "How many spools are on your paper. What does this word say? Why is it written here? Could you use it to tell about the spools? Where would be a good place to write it on your paper? That's a fine job. Let me see you do this next one."

Tell me about your workjob.

What did you write on your paper? How did you know what to write? Where did you find the words to use? What do these words tell about?

Show me the answercard that your paper tells about. Read your paper to me, please.

Show me with your fingers what this numeral you've written means. Are you holding up the same number of fingers as the numeral represents?

Are there more spools or more fingers, or what? Why?

6″ x 6″ squares of cardboard.
Objects to form sets.
Marking pen.
Epoxy glue.
Paper.
Crayons.
Container for cards.

Trees and Apples

Skills Forming sets of objects; counting; making comparisons; combining groups.

The child places apples on each tree until the amount matches the numeral on the tree trunk.

You might ask the child, "What is this numeral, Marvin? Are there that many apples on the tree? Can you fix it so there are enough apples?"

What did you do with the apples?
How many apples are on this tree?
Are there more trees or more apples?
These two trees have how many apples between them?
Which tree has the fewest apples? The most?
How many apples would need to fall down to leave only two apples on
   this tree?
I see a mistake on this tree. Do you see it? Can you fix it?

Tagboard piece 6″ x 9″.
Marking pen in brown to make tree trunks.
Self-adhesive labels on which to write numerals.
Green felt to make tree tops.
Apples cut from red felt.
Container for apples.
Container for answerboards and boxed apples.

The Beans

104

The child determines how many beans he wishes to remove from each bunch. After removing them, he counts to see how many are left and records the operation. When he has finished, the child replaces the beans on the vine before putting the boards away.

The activity might be discussed as follows: "How many beans would you like to take away from this bunch? Okay. How many do you think will be left? Try it and see. Were you right? Good. Can you write what you did?"

How many beans did you have to start with here? And how many are there now? What happened in between? How many did you take off? If you put them back on, how many would you have? Show me.

Which group has the most beans on the vine? Which has the least?

How many beans did you take away from here? And here?

Is there any place where you took all the beans off? What would happen if you did? How many would be left?

How many beans would be left if you removed zero beans from this group? How can that be?

Plastic beans whose pods can be easily removed and replaced on the stem.
6″ x 9″ pieces of 1/8″ plywood on which the beans are secured with heavy staples.
Paper and pencil.
Container for the bean boards.

The Money Game

Skills Making comparisons; observing the relationship of one quantity to another; counting; identifying common coins; identifying equivalent coin values; developing a respect for property.

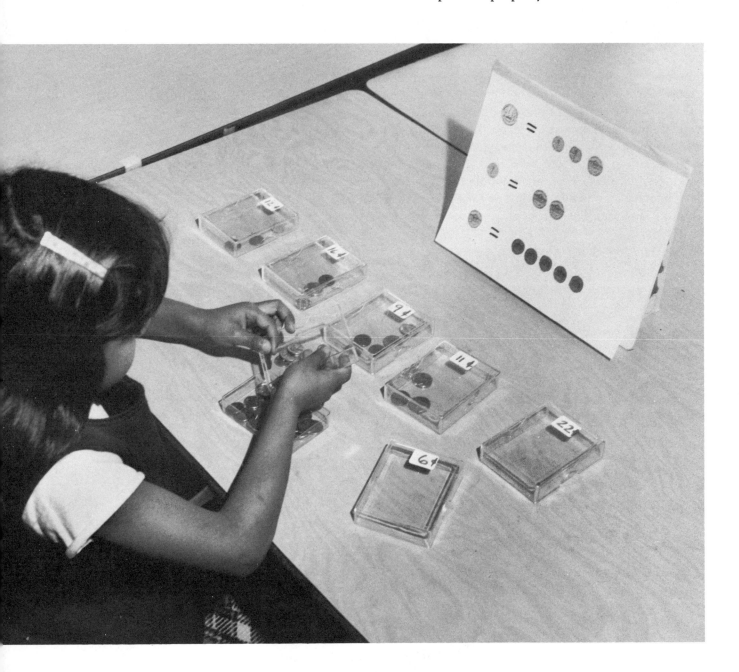

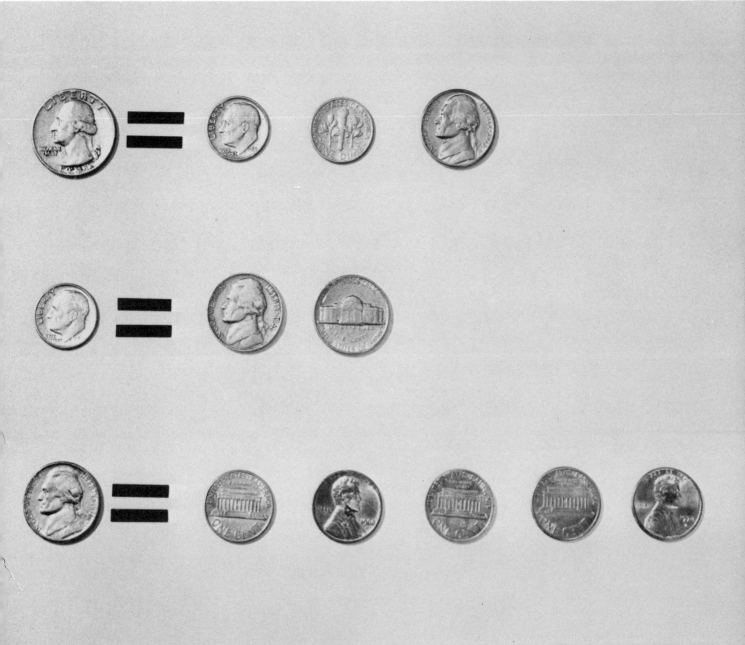

107

The child places the appropriate number of coins into each box. When he has finished, the child matches the silver coins to a matching board and places the pennies in a plastic cylinder.

Children will create different combinations. Some children working with the eleven cent box, for example, will put in two nickles and one penny, while another child will put in one dime and one penny. Still another child will use 11 pennies. It is very interesting to notice how children solve the problem when they near the end of the workjob with perhaps only two boxes left to fill and find they have only silver coins to fill a three cent and a nine cent box.

You might ask the child, "How many cents go into this box? Can you count out that much?"

Tell me about the money boxes, Charles.

Which coin do we call a nickel? How many cents is it worth? Which is a dime? How many cents is it worth? Without looking, can you remember which is larger, a nickel or a dime? Which is worth more?

Tell me about the coins in this box.

Which box has the most money in it? Which one has the most pennies? Is it worth the most—could you buy more with the money in this box than with the money in any other?

Small boxes.
Marking pen for writing amounts of money.
Labels.
Real or play money.
Container for money.
Container for boxes.
Reference card showing equivalent coin value (see page 107 for picture to cut out).

Fences

110

The child puts the animals into the fences. Then he records the number of each animal in each fence. For example, one may have five horses and three cows and the child would record 5 + 3 = 8.

You might discuss the activity as follows: "Pretend you are a cowboy going on a round-up. How many animals will you put in this fence?"

Tell me about your work, Amalia.
How did you decide how many animals to put in each fence?
Are there any fences that have the same number of animals inside?
Which fence has fewer than six animals inside it?
How many of each kind of animals are inside this fence?
If three of these animals got away, how many would be left? What would happen if two animals broke out of their fence and got into this fence?

4" x 4" pieces of tagboard.
Popsicle sticks glued together to form fences.
Small animals of two types, such as cows and horses, to be placed inside fences.
Paper and pencil.
Container for animals.
Container for fences and boxed animals.

Airplanes and Hangars

Skills Counting; adding; experience with the symmetrical property of equality; matching.

The child works out the addition problem placed on the wings and taxis each airplane into the appropriate hanger to show the answers.

Extra airplanes might be available on which the child could write his own combinations with a crayon. The crayon is wiped off with a soft cloth when the child is finished.

ACTIVITY

The activity might be discussed as follows: "If you add these two numbers together, how many do you get? Good for you, Howard! Can you taxi the airplane into the hanger it should go in?"

GETTING STARTED

What did you do with the airplanes and hangars?
How can *both* these planes be in the same hangar?
I am looking at a hangar that has three planes inside. Each one totals seven. What colors are the planes?
I am thinking of a hangar for 4 + 1. Point to it, please.
I see an airplane in hangar 7 that doesn't belong. Can you find it and put it into its hangar?

IDEAS FOR
FOLLOW-UP DISCUSSION

Tagboard rectangles 8″ × 18″ taped onto an 8″ × 10″ piece of cardboard to make each hanger.
Marking pen to write numerals.
Small toy airplanes with combinations written across their wing spans.
Container for airplanes.
Container for hangars and boxed airplanes.

MATERIALS

Hide 'n' Go Seek

Skills Counting; subtracting, withdrawing a part from the whole; making abstractions; strengthening memory; recording experience with mathematical symbols.

114

The child decides the number he wants to work with and sets that number on the table where he can see it. He puts as many blocks into *each* pie tin as the numeral says. When he has finished, he places some of the blocks for each pie tin *under* the tin and the others on top. When a child finishes this procedure he writes on a piece of paper (placed in front of each pie tin) how many blocks he thinks are hiding underneath. For example, if a child is working with number 6 and has four blocks on top of a particular pie tin, he thinks about how many blocks must be under this pie tin since the total number of blocks is six. The child would write two. $4 + ? = 6; 4 + 2 = 6$.

The activity might be discussed as follows: "Select a numeral you would enjoy working with, Gina. Okay, put that many blocks into each pie tin. (When she finishes) Now put *some* blocks from this tin underneath and leave some on top. Good! Now do this for all the blocks and try to leave a different number of blocks on top of each one. (When finished) Write down a guess for how many blocks you think are under each one!

How many blocks did you count into each pie tin?

How many blocks are there in each set—on top and underneath?

How many blocks are on top of this pie tin? How many do you think are hidden underneath? Peek and see if you're right. Were you?

Why do you think there are four blocks under this pie tin? How can you know if they're hidden and you can't count them? Is this magic?

10 pie plates from small meat or fruit pies.

1″ cubes.

Paper.

Crayon.

Plastic numerals 4, 5, 6, 7, 8, and 9.

Container for numerals.

Container for cubes.

Container for pie tins, boxed numerals, and boxed cubes.